LET'S TALK ABOUT

SAYING NO

by Joy Berry • Illustrated by Maggie Smith

Joy Berry Enterprises

Hello, my name is Casper.

I live with Tonya.

Sometimes Tonya should say no,
and sometimes she shouldn't.

You should say no when you are asked to do something you know you shouldn't do.

I get my toys before my bath begins.

I do not choose toys that

could get ruined in the water.

I choose my bath toys carefully.

You should say no when you are asked to do something you aren't able to do.

You should say no when people ask you to do something you don't need or want to do.

You should say no when people ask you to give them something that you don't need or want to give.

You should say no when someone offers to do something you don't want them to do.

You should also say no when someone offers to give you something you don't want.

You should say no when you are asked if you understand something you don't understand.

You should say no when you are asked if you agree, and you don't agree.

You should say no when you are asked if you like something you don't like.

You should say no when you are asked
to feel an emotion you don't feel.

You should *not* say no when you are asked
to do something that will prevent
you from being hurt,
others from being hurt, or
things from being damaged
or destroyed.

You should *not* say no when you are asked to do something that you are supposed to do.

You should *not* say no when it is a lie.

It is important to be courteous whenever you tell a person no.

Speak calmly and try not to say mean things.

Saying no will be more acceptable if you say it in a nice way. Here are some kind ways to say no:

No, thank you. No, maybe some other time. I am sorry, but no.

It's best for everyone when you say no at the right time and in a kind way.

Let's talk about . . . **Joy Berry!**

Joy Berry knows kids. As the inventor of self-help books for kids, she has written over 250 books that teach children about taking responsibility for themselves and their actions. With sales of over 80 million copies, Joy's books have helped millions of parents and their kids.

Through interesting stories that kids can relate to, Joy Berry's *Let's Talk About* books explain how to handle even the toughest situations and emotions. Written in a clear, simple style and illustrated with bright, humorous pictures, the *Let's Talk About* books are fun, informative, and they really work!

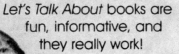

Printed in the USA
CPSIA information can be obtained
at www.ICGtesting.com
LVHW050325300923
759526LV00009B/1479